BARACK OBAMA

QUOTES TO LIVE BY

Published by OH!
20 Mortimer Street
London W1T 3JW

Text © 2020 OH
Design © 2020 OH
First published by Carlton Books 2019

A CIP catalogue for this book is available from the British Library.

ISBN 978 1 78739 306 6

Editor: Alex Lemon
Designer: Lucy Palmer

Printed in Dubai

10 9 8 7 6 5 4

CONTENTS

1

HOPE & CHANGE

The stylized poster bearing only Barack Obama's face and the word "Hope" became the standout image of Obama's 2008 presidential bid. His campaign also used the slogan "Change we can believe in". These words and sentiments set the tone – and a high bar – for what voters expected from Obama's presidency.

"

Change will not come if we wait for some other person or some other time. We are the ones we've been waiting for. We are the change that we seek.

"

Speech post-nominating contests,
Chicago, Illinois, US, 5 February, 2008

"

Hope is not blind optimism. It's not ignoring the enormity of the tasks ahead or the roadblocks that stand in our path. It's not sitting on the sidelines or shirking from a fight.

"

Iowa caucus victory speech, US,
January 2008

66

No matter what obstacles stand
in our way, nothing can stand in
the way of the power of millions of
voices calling for change. **99**

Democratic Party presidential primary campaign,
Goffstown, New Hampshire, US, January 2008

"

If one voice can change a room, then it can change a city, and if it can change a city, it can change a state, and if it can change a state, it can change a nation, and if it can change a nation, it can change the world. **"**

Hillary Clinton campaign rally, Durham,
New Hampshire, US, November 2016

66

Yes we can, to justice and equality. Yes we can, to opportunity and prosperity. Yes we can heal this nation. Yes we can repair this world. Yes we can.

99

Democratic Party presidential primary campaign, Goffstown, New Hampshire, US, January 2008

66

Don't shortchange the future because
of fear of the present. **99**

G20 news conference, Downing Street, London,
UK, April 2009.

66

While the future is unknowable, the winds always blow in the direction of human progress.

99

Departure ceremony, Accra, Ghana, July 2009

66

Hope is the bedrock of this nation.
The belief that our destiny will not
be written for us, but by us, by all
those men and women who are not
content to settle for the world as it is,
who have the courage to remake the
world as it should be.
99

Iowa caucus victory speech, US,
January 2008

66

Progress will come in fits and starts.
It's not always a straight line. It's not
always a smooth path.

99

Re-election victory speech, Chicago, Illinois,
US, November 2012

66

One voice can change a room.

99

Final campaign rally, Des Moines, Iowa,
US, November 2012

66

Making your mark on the world is hard. If it were easy, everybody would do it. But it's not. It takes patience, it takes commitment and it comes with plenty of failure along the way. **99**

Northwestern University commencement, Evanston, Illinois, US, June 2006

66
We did not come to fear the future.
We came here to shape it. **99**

Joint session of Congress on healthcare, Washington
DC, US, September 2009

66

The best way to not feel hopeless is to get up and do something. Don't wait for good things to happen to you. If you go out and make some good things happen, you will fill the world with hope, you will fill yourself with hope.

99

Dreams from My Father, Barack Obama's autobiography, 1995

66

To anyone out there who's hurting:
it's not a sign of weakness to ask for
help, it's a sign of strength. **99**

On signing the Clay Hunt Suicide Prevention for
American Veterans Act, Washington DC, US,
February 2015

66

We choose hope over fear. We see the future not as something out of our control, but as something we can shape for the better through concerted and collective effort. **99**

UN General Assembly, New York, US,
September 2014

66

Too often what I see is wonderful activism that highlights a problem, but then people feel so passionately and are so invested in the purity of their position that they never take that next step and say, okay, well, now I've got to sit down and try to actually get something done. 99

Town hall with UK young leaders, London, UK, April 2016

"
Change does not come *from* Washington, but *to* Washington.

Let Freedom Ring ceremony on the 50th anniversary of the March on Washington, US, August 2013

"

66

We shouldn't downplay how far we've come. That would do a disservice to all those who spent their lives fighting for justice. At the same time, there's still a lot of work we need to do to improve the prospects of women and girls here and around the world. **99**

Column "This is what a feminist looks like" for *Glamour* magazine, August 2016

66

You are standing in a moment where
your capacity to shape this world
is unmatched. What an incredible
privilege that is. **99**

Town hall with UK young leaders, London,
UK, April 2016

66

I do have one final ask of you as your president – the same thing I asked when you took a chance on me eight years ago. I am asking you to believe. Not in my ability to bring about change, but in yours. **99**

Farewell address, Chicago, Illinois, US,
January 2017

66

Fighting for change that you may not live to see, but that your children will live to see. That's what this is all about. That's what we are all about.

Town hall with UK young leaders,
London, UK, April 2016

❝

I think that change happens,
typically not because somebody
on high decides that it's going to
happen, but rather because at a
grassroots level enough people
come together that they force the
system to change. **❞**

Conversation with *The Undefeated*, North Carolina
A&T State University, US, October 2016

66

The arc of the moral universe may
bend towards justice, but it doesn't
bend on its own.

99

Let Freedom Ring ceremony on the 50th
anniversary of the March on Washington,
US, August 2013

66

The absence of hope can rot a
society from within.

99

Nobel Prize lecture, Oslo, Norway,
December 2009

66
There has never been anything false about hope. **99**

Democratic Party presidential primary campaign, Goffstown, New Hampshire, US, January 2008

❝

Power comes from appealing to people's hopes, not people's fears.

Speech at the University of Yangon, Rangoon, Burma, November 2012

❞

"
Hope is that stubborn thing inside us that insists, despite all the evidence to the contrary, that something better awaits us, so long as we have the courage to keep reaching, to keep working, to keep fighting. **"**

Re-election victory speech, Chicago, Illinois, US, November 2012

"
Change has never been quick.
Change has never been simple,
or without controversy. Change
depends on persistence. Change
requires determination. **"**

Martin Luther King, Jr. Memorial dedication,
Washington DC, US, October 2011

66

The young are unconstrained by habits of fear, unconstrained by the conventions of what is. **99**

Let Freedom Ring ceremony on the 50th anniversary of the March on Washington, US, August 2013

66

It always seems impossible until it
is done.
99

Memorial service for former South African
President Nelson Mandela, Johannesburg, South
Africa, December 2013

66

Freedom is not an accident. Progress is not an accident. Democracy is not an accident. These are things that have to be fought for. **99**

US Army Garrison Yongsan, Seoul, Republic of Korea, April 2014

66

Positive change is achieved not through passion alone, but through patient and persistent effort. **99**

Young Southeast Asian Leaders Initiative, Kuala Lumpur, Malaysia, April 2014

66

One of the best indicators of whether a country will succeed is how it treats its women, when women have an education, when women have a job – their children are more likely to get an education, their families are healthier and more prosperous, their communities and countries do better.

Speech on the Sustainable Development Goals, United Nations, New York, US, September 2015 **99**

66

With hard work and with hope,
change is always within our reach.

Young Leaders of the Americas town hall,
Kingston, Jamaica, April 2015

99

66

Civil society is the conscience of our countries. It's the catalyst of change. It's why strong nations don't fear active citizens. Strong nations embrace and support and empower active citizens.

99

Civil Society Forum, Panama City, Panama, April 2015

“

You can't be complacent and
accept the world just as it is. You
have to imagine what the world
might be and then push and work
toward that future. **”**

Address to the Kenyan people, Nairobi,
Kenya, July 2015

2
MEANING &
PURPOSE

Becoming President of the United States is no easy task. Becoming the first black President of the United States is even harder. Clear in Obama's path through politics was his drive, intent and persistence – motivated by a strong sense of what he wanted to achieve and what he held dear.

66

Focusing your life solely on making a buck shows a certain poverty of ambition. It asks too little of yourself. And it will leave you unfulfilled. **99**

Northwestern University commencement, Evanston, Illinois, US, June 2006

66

It's only when you hitch your wagon
to something larger than yourself that
you realize your true potential. **99**

Northwestern University commencement,
Evanston, Illinois, US, June 2006

66

[W]e may not look the same and we may not have come from the same place, but we all want to move in the same direction – towards a better future for our children and our grandchildren.

99

Democratic Party presidential primary campaign, Philadelphia, Pennsylvania, US, March 2008

"
We have a choice. We can shape our future, or let events shape it for us. And if we want to succeed, we can't fall back on the stale debates and old divides that won't move us forward. **"**

G20 news conference, Downing Street,
London, UK, April 2009

66

If you are living your life to the fullest, you will fail, you will stumble, you will screw up, you will fall down. But it will make you stronger, and you'll get it right the next time, or the time after that, or the time after that. **99**

Ohio State University commencement, Columbus, Ohio, US, May 2013

66

Greatness is never a given. It must
be earned.

99

Inauguration address, Washington DC,
US, January 2009

"

The real test is not whether you avoid failure, because you won't. It's whether you let it harden or shame you into inaction, or whether you learn from it; whether you choose to persevere. **"**

Northwestern University commencement,
Evanston, Illinois, US, June 2006

66

The cynics may be the loudest
voices but, I promise you, they will
accomplish the least. 99

Ohio State University commencement, Columbus,
Ohio, US, May 2015

66

Challenge yourself. Take some risks in your life.

99

Northwestern University commencement, Evanston, Illinois, US, June 2006

❝ Nothing in life that's worth anything is easy. **❞**

State of the Union address, the White House, US, January 2014

66

Our individual salvation depends on collective salvation … Thinking only about yourself, fulfilling your immediate wants and needs, betrays a poverty of ambition. **99**

Wesleyan University graduation ceremony, Middletown, Connecticut, US, May 2008

"

The future rewards those who press on ... I don't have time to feel sorry for myself. I don't have time to complain. I'm going to press on.

"

Congressional Black Caucus Foundation annual Phoenix Awards dinner, Washington DC, US, September 2011

66

You can't let your failures define you
– you have to let them teach you.
You have to let them show you what
to do differently next time.
99

Back to school speech, Wakefield High School,
Arlington, Virginia, US, September 2009

"

We respect human dignity, even when we're threatened … We condemn the persecution of women, or religious minorities, or people who are lesbian, gay, bisexual, or transgender. We do these things not only because they are the right thing to do, but because ultimately they will make us safer.

"

State of the Union address, Washington DC, US, January 2015

66

One of the benefits of defeat is to take some of the vanity out of what it is that you're trying to achieve. And you start reminding yourself part of your strength comes from realizing, 'Oh, this isn't about me, this about what I'm doing for somebody else'.

99

Conversation with *The Undefeated*,
North Carolina A&T State University,
US, October 2016

❝ Love comes more naturally to the human heart. Let's remember that truth, let's see it as our North Star, let's be joyful in our struggle to make that truth manifest here on earth. **❞**

Nelson Mandela annual lecture,
Johannesburg, South Africa, July 2018

66

Our common prosperity will be advanced by allowing all humanity – men and women – to reach their full potential. **99**

A New Beginning speech, Cairo University, Egypt, June 2009

"

Cultivating empathy, challenging yourself, persevering in the face of adversity – these are the qualities that I've found to be important in my own life.

"

Northwestern University commencement, Evanston, Illinois, US, June 2006

"
All of us share this world for but a brief moment in time. The question is whether we spend that time focused on what pushes us apart, or whether we commit ourselves to an effort – a sustained effort – to find common ground. **"**

A New Beginning speech, Cairo University, Egypt, June 2009

66

As the world grows smaller, you
might think it would be easier for
human beings to recognize how
similar we are. **99**

Nobel Prize lecture, Oslo, Norway,
December 2009

66

Freedom is not given, it must be won, through struggle and discipline, persistence and faith. **99**

Let Freedom Ring ceremony on the 50th anniversary of the March on Washington, US, August 2013

66

We are more free when all people can pursue their own happiness.

99

Speech at the Brandenburg Gate, Berlin, Germany, June 2013

66

Prosperity without freedom is just another form of poverty.

99

Speech at the University of Indonesia in Jakarta, Indonesia, November 2010

"
What makes you a man isn't the ability to conceive a child; it's having the courage to raise one.

"

State of the Union address, Washington DC, US, February 2013

66
We know this country cannot accomplish great things if we pursue nothing greater than our own individual ambition. **99**

Ohio State University commencement, Columbus, Ohio, US, May 2013

66

When we turn not from each other, or on each other, but towards one another, and we find that we do not walk alone. That's where courage comes from.

99

Let Freedom Ring ceremony on the 50th anniversary of the March on Washington, US, August 2013

"

If you give up on the idea that your voice can make a difference, then other voices will fill the void. **"**

Democratic Party presidential nomination acceptance speech, Charlotte, North Carolina, US, September 2012

66

If you're only thinking about you,
then your world is small; if you're
thinking about others, then your
world gets bigger. **99**

Young Southeast Asian Leaders Initiative, Kuala
Lumpur, Malaysia, April 2014

66

We can always understand that most important decision – the decision we make when we find our common humanity in one another. That's always available to us, that choice.

99

University of Cape Town, South Africa, June 2013

66

Vision is important, but then you also have to have the persistence to keep working to make progress. And I always tell young people to have big dreams, but then also be willing to work for those dreams. It's not going to come right away. **99**

Young Southeast Asian Leaders Initiative, Kuala Lumpur, Malaysia, November 2015

66

Tell us what you are for, not just what you're against. That way we can have a vigorous and meaningful debate.

99

Speech on economic mobility, Washington DC, US, December 2013

66

The job of a leader is not to try to do everything yourself, but it's to try to organize people, each of whom have different talents and skills. Make sure that they are joined in a common vision about what needs to get done. 99

Young Southeast Asian Leaders Initiative, Kuala Lumpur, Malaysia, November 2015

66

You have to be willing to take some risks and do some hard things in order to be a leader. A leader is not just a name, a title, and privileges and perks.

99

Young African Leaders Initiative Presidential Summit, Washington DC, US, August 2015

66

Don't let people talk you into doing the safe thing. Listen to what's inside of you and decide what it is that you care about so much that you're willing to risk it all.

99

Northwestern University commencement, Evanston, Illinois, US, June 2006

"

You do not lift yourself up by holding
somebody else down.

Young African Leaders Initiative Presidential
Summit, Washington DC, US, August 2015

"

66

If you're walking down the right path
and you're willing to keep walking,
eventually you'll make progress. **99**

Farewell address, Chicago, Illinois, US,
January 2017

3
FAITH &
BELIEF

Barack Obama has spoken often about his devout Christian faith and its role in his life and decisions. He's also been clear and vocal about his underlying beliefs in humanity and in human possibility, and what it means to be human, facing struggles with ourselves and each other every day.

66

My parents shared not only an improbable love, they shared an abiding faith in the possibilities of this nation. **99**

Democratic National Convention, Boston, Massachusetts, US, July 2004

66

You can't give up your passion if things don't work right away. You can't lose heart, or grow cynical if there are twists and turns on your journey. **99**

Ohio State University commencement, Columbus, Ohio, US, May 2014

"

Part of my job as a Christian is to recognize that I may not always be right, that God doesn't speak to me alone, and that the only way that I could live effectively with people who have different beliefs and different faiths is if we have a civil society that is, in fact, civil. **"**

Interview for ABC's *This Week* with George Stephanopoulos, August 2004

66

Hope in the face of difficulty,
hope in the face of uncertainty, the
audacity of hope: In the end, that is
God's greatest gift to us, the bedrock
of this nation, a belief in things not
seen, a belief that there are better
days ahead. **99**

Democratic National Convention, Boston,
Massachusetts, US, July 2004

66

That is our unyielding faith – that
in the face of impossible odds,
people who love their country can
change it. **99**

Formal announcement of seeking the Democratic
nomination for President, February 2007

66 The only thing that's the end of the world is the end of the world. **99**

Final press conference, Washington DC, US, January 2017

66

As far as we've come, all too often
we are still boxed in by stereotypes
about how men and women should
behave. **99**

Column "This is what a feminist looks like" for
Glamour magazine, August 2016

“

You have to believe in facts.
Without facts there is no basis for
cooperation. **"**

Nelson Mandela annual lecture, Johannesburg,
South Africa, July 2018

66

Gender stereotypes affect all of us,
regardless of our gender, gender
identity, or sexual orientation. **99**

Column "This is what a feminist looks like" for
Glamour magazine, August 2016

66

It should be the power of our vote,
not the size of our bank account,
that drives our democracy. **99**

State of the Union address, Washington DC,
US, January 2014

66

Forcing people to adhere to outmoded, rigid notions of identity isn't good for anybody – men, women, gay, straight, transgender, or otherwise. These stereotypes limit our ability to simply be ourselves.

Column "This is what a feminist looks like" for *Glamour* magazine, August 2016

66

We need all our young people
to know that Clara Barton and
Lucretia Mott and Sojourner Truth
and Eleanor Roosevelt and Dorothy
Height, those aren't just for Women's
History Month. They're the authors of
our history, women who shaped their
destiny. **99**

United States of Women Summit, Washington DC,
US, June 2016

66

I believe in a vision of equality and justice and freedom and multiracial democracy built on the premise that all people are created equal and they're endowed by our Creator certain inalienable rights.

Nelson Mandela annual lecture, Johannesburg, South Africa, July 2018

99

> **"**
> The interests we share as human beings are far more powerful than the forces that drive us apart. **"**

A New Beginning speech, Cairo University, Egypt, June 2009

"

I am living testimony to the moral force of non-violence. I know there's nothing weak, nothing passive, nothing naïve in the creed and lives of Gandhi and King. **"**

Nobel Prize lecture, Oslo, Norway, December 2009

66

We may not be able to stop all evil
in the world, but I know that how we
treat one another is entirely up to us.

99

Memorial service for the victims of the
shooting in Tucson, Arizona, US, January 2011

“

My faith is one that admits some doubt.

”

Interview for ABC's *This Week* with George Stephanopoulos, August 2004

66

Fear is the force that stands between human beings and their dreams.

Speech at the University of Yangon, Rangoon, Burma, November 2012

99

"

It's easy to absorb all kinds of messages from society about masculinity and come to believe that there's a right way and a wrong way to be a man. **"**

Column "This is what a feminist looks like" for *Glamour* magazine, August 2016

66 None of us are fully free when others in the human family remain shackled by poverty or disease or oppression. **99**

University of Cape Town, South Africa, June 2013

66

Our success should depend not on accident of birth but the strength of our work ethic and the scope of our dreams. **99**

State of the Union address, Washington DC, US, January 2014

66 Traditionally, wealth was defined
by land and natural resources.
Today the most important resource is
between our ears. **99**

Young Southeast Asian Leaders Initiative,
Kuala Lumpur, Malaysia, April 2014

66

Belief in permanent religious war is
the misguided refuge of extremists
who cannot build or create anything,
and therefore peddle only fanaticism
and hate. **99**

UN General Assembly, New York, US,
September 2014

"

If we sacrifice liberty in the name of
security, we risk losing both. **"**

Address to the people of Africa, Addis Ababa,
Ethiopia, July 2015

66

No external power can bring
about a transformation of hearts and
minds.

99

UN General Assembly, New York, US,
September 2014

66

The peace we seek in the world begins in human hearts. And it finds its glorious expression when we look beyond any differences in religion or tribe, and rejoice in the beauty of every soul.

99

Address to the people of India, Mumbai, India, January 2015

66

Every one of us is equal. Every one of us has worth. Every one of us matters.

99

Address to the people of Africa, Addis Ababa, Ethiopia, July 2015

66

A nation ringed by walls would only imprison itself.

99

71st session of the United Nations General Assembly, September 2016

4

POLITICS & PRINCIPLES

Barack Obama cut his political teeth as a grassroots activist in poor neighbourhoods of Chicago in the 1980s. When he swept to victory in 2008, he did so on a platform of change, pledging to bring not just new policies but new practices and a new attitude to Washington.

66

Politics has become so bitter and
partisan, so gummed up by money
and influence, that we can't tackle
the big problems that demand
solutions. **99**

Statement announcing his exploration of
presidential candidacy, January 2007

"

If you don't have any fresh ideas, then you use stale tactics to scare the voters. If you don't have a record to run on, then you paint your opponent as someone people should run from. You make a big election about small things. **"**

Democratic Party nomination acceptance speech, Denver, Colorado, US, August 2008

"

My attitude is that if the economy's good for folks from the bottom up, it's gonna be good for everybody … I think when you spread the wealth around, it's good for everybody.

"

Comments on campaign, Holland, Ohio, US, October 2008

66

We cannot solve the challenges
of our time unless we solve them
together. **99**

Democratic Party presidential primary campaign,
Philadelphia, Pennsylvania, US, March 2008

66

Let us resist the temptation to fall back on the same partisanship and pettiness and immaturity that has poisoned our politics for so long.

99

Election victory speech, Chicago, Illinois, US, November 2008

66

No country is going to create wealth
if its leaders exploit the economy to
enrich themselves. 99

Address to the Ghanaian Parliament, Accra,
Ghana, July 2009

66

You can disagree with a
certain policy without demonizing
the person who espouses it. **99**

University of Michigan commencement
address, Ann Arbour, Michigan, US, May 2010

66

My job is to solve problems, not to stand on the sidelines and carp and gripe. **99**

Speech at Maycomb Community College, Warren, Michigan, US, July 2009

66

I think we should talk more about our empathy deficit – the ability to put ourselves in someone else's shoes; to see the world through those who are different from us – the child who's hungry, the laid-off steelworker, the immigrant woman cleaning your dorm room. **99**

Northwestern University commencement, Evanston, Illinois, US, June 2006

66

When our government is spoken
of as some menacing, threatening
foreign entity, it ignores the fact that
in our democracy, government is us.
We, the people.

99

University of Michigan commencement address,
Ann Arbour, Michigan, US, May 2010

"

The strongest democracies flourish
from frequent and lively debate, but
they endure when people of every
background and belief find a way
to set aside smaller differences in
service of a greater purpose. **"**

First presidential press conference,
Washington DC, US, February 2009

66

Empowering women isn't just the
right thing to do – it's the smart thing
to do. When women succeed,
nations are more safe, more secure,
and more prosperous.   **99**

Speech on International Women's Day,
March 2013

66

Politics has never been for the thin skinned or the faint of heart, and if you enter the arena, you should expect to get roughed up. **99**

University of Michigan commencement address,
Ann Arbour, Michigan, US, May 2010

" We live in a culture that discourages empathy. A culture that too often tells us our principal goal in life is to be rich, thin, young, famous, safe, and entertained. A culture where those in power too often encourage these selfish impulses. **"**

Northwestern University commencement, Evanston, Illinois, US, June 2006

66

The practice of listening to opposing
views is essential for effective
citizenship. It is essential for our
democracy.   **99**

University of Michigan commencement address,
Ann Arbour, Michigan, US, May 2010

66

The strongest weapon against hateful speech is not repression; it is more speech.

99

UN General Assembly, New York, US, September 2012

" Every woman should be able to go about her day – to walk the streets or ride the bus – and be safe, and be treated with respect and dignity. She deserves that. **"**

Address to the people of India, Mumbai, India, January 2015

"
The role of citizen in a democracy does not end with your vote. **"**

Re-election victory speech, Chicago, Illinois, US, November 2012

66

The value of social movements and activism is to get you at the table, get you in the room, and then to start trying to figure out how is this problem going to be solved. **99**

Town hall with UK young leaders, London, UK, April 2016

66

History also shows the power of
fear. History shows the lasting
hold of greed and the desire to
dominate others in the minds of men.
Especially men. **99**

Nelson Mandela annual lecture, Johannesburg,
South Africa, July 2018

66

War itself is never glorious, and we must never trumpet it as such. **99**

Nobel Prize lecture, Oslo, Norway, December 2009

66

Politicians have always lied, but it used to be if you caught them lying they'd be like, 'Oh man'. Now they just keep on lying. **99**

Nelson Mandela annual lecture, Johannesburg, South Africa, July 2018

66

The belief that peace is desirable
is rarely enough to achieve it.
Peace requires responsibility. Peace
entails sacrifice. **99**

Nobel Prize lecture, Oslo, Norway,
December 2009

" The most important office in a democracy is the office of citizen – not President, not Speaker, but citizen. **"**

Speech at the University of Yangon, Rangoon, Burma, November 2012

66

Peace is not merely the absence of visible conflict. Only a just peace based on the inherent rights and dignity of every individual can truly be lasting.

99

Nobel Prize lecture, Oslo, Norway, December 2009

66

For all the power of militaries, for
all the authority of governments, it is
citizens who choose whether to be
defined by a wall, or whether to tear
it down. **99**

Speech at the Brandenburg Gate, Berlin,
Germany, June 2013

66

There is no speech that justifies
mindless violence. There are
no words that excuse the killing
of innocents. **99**

UN General Assembly, New York, US,
September 2012

66

Our country cannot succeed when
a shrinking few do very well and a
growing many barely make it. **99**

Second inaugural address, Washington DC,
US, January 2013

66

We can't expect to solve our problems if all we do is tear each other down. **99**

University of Michigan commencement address, Ann Arbour, Michigan, US, May 2010

66

Rising inequality and declining mobility are bad for our democracy. Ordinary folks can't write massive campaign checks or hire high-priced lobbyists and lawyers to secure policies that tilt the playing field in their favour at everyone else's expense.

99

Speech on economic mobility, Washington DC, US, December 2013

66

We can't condemn future
generations to a planet that is
beyond fixing. **99**

Young Southeast Asian Leaders Initiative, Kuala
Lumpur, Malaysia, April 2014

66

Justice is not only the absence
of oppression, it is the presence
of opportunity.

99

NAACP Conference, Philadelphia, Pennsylvania,
US, July 2015

66

Democracies don't stop just with elections; they also depend on strong institutions and a vibrant civil society, and open political space, and tolerance of people who are different than you. **99**

Young Southeast Asian Leaders Initiative, Kuala Lumpur, Malaysia, April 2014

"

What's our excuse today for not voting? How do we so casually discard the right for which so many fought? How do we so fully give away our power, our voice? **"**

50th Anniversary of the Selma to Montgomery Marches, Selma, Alabama, US, March 2015

66

When we don't pay close attention
to the decisions made by our
leaders, when we fail to educate
ourselves about the major issues
of the day, when we choose not
to make our voices and opinions
heard, that's when democracy
breaks down. **99**

University of Michigan commencement address,
Ann Arbour, Michigan, US, May 2010

"

If you want more authority, then you also have to be more responsible. You can't wear the crown if you can't bear the cross.

"

Young African Leaders Initiative Presidential Summit, Washington DC, US, August 2015

66

One of the things that leadership
requires is saying things even
when it's uncomfortable, even when
it's unpopular – especially when
it's unpopular.   **99**

Young Southeast Asian Leaders Initiative,
Rangoon, Burma, November 2014

66

Treating women as second-class
citizens is a bad tradition. **99**

Address to the Kenyan people, Nairobi,
Kenya, July 2015

"

Vilification and over-the-top rhetoric closes the door to the possibility of compromise. It undermines democratic deliberation. It prevents learning. **"**

University of Michigan commencement address, Ann Arbour, Michigan, US, May 2010

66

A world in which one per cent of humanity controls as much wealth as the other 99 per cent will never be stable.

99

71st session of the United Nations General Assembly, New York City, US, September 2016

5

AMERICA

Barack Obama was born in Hawaii to a black Kenyan father and a white American mother, and partially raised in Indonesia. He married the daughter of working-class parents, who can trace her ancestry to slaves. These experiences and histories helped form Obama's vision of an inclusive, equal America, strengthened by its differences.

" There is not a liberal America and a conservative America – there is the United States of America. There is not a Black America and a White America and Latino America and Asian America – there's the United States of America. **"**

Democratic National Convention, Boston, Massachusetts, US, July 2004

66

Whatever we once were, we
are no longer just a Christian nation;
we are also a Jewish nation, a
Muslim nation, a Buddhist nation,
a Hindu nation, and a nation of
non-believers.

99

Call to Renewal's "Building a Covenant for a
New America" conference, Washington DC,
US, June 2006

66

For all the progress we have made, there are times when the land of our dreams recedes from us – when we are lost, wandering spirits, content with our suspicions and our angers, our long-held grudges and petty disputes, our frantic diversions and tribal allegiances. **99**

Dr Martin Luther King, Jr. National Memorial groundbreaking ceremony, November 2006

66

We have never been just a collection of individuals or a collection of red states and blue states. We are, and always will be, the United States of America.

99

Election victory speech, Chicago, Illinois, US, November 2008

"

The cynics, the lobbyists, the special interests, who've turned government into only a game they can afford to play. They write the checks while you get stuck with the bill. They get access while you get to write a letter. **"**

Formal announcement of seeking the Democratic nomination for President, February 2007

66

We've got a tragic history when it comes to race in this country. A lot of pent-up anger and mistrust and bitterness. This country wants to move beyond these kinds of things. **99**

Democratic nomination campaign, Plainfield, Indiana, US, March 2008

66

This union may never be perfect, but generation after generation has shown that it can always be perfected. **99**

Democratic Party presidential primary campaign, Philadelphia, Pennsylvania, US, March 2008

66

If the financial crisis taught us anything, it's that we cannot have a thriving Wall Street while Main Street suffers.

99

Election victory speech, Chicago, Illinois, US, November 2008

"

I believe in American exceptionalism, just as I suspect that the Brits believe in British exceptionalism and the Greeks believe in Greek exceptionalism.

"

News conference, Palais de la Musique et des Congrès in Strasbourg, France, April 2009

66

Our patchwork heritage is a
strength, not a weakness.

Inauguration address, Washington DC,
US, January 2009

99

"

When we measure our greatness as a nation by how far the stock market rises or falls, instead of how many opportunities we've opened up for America's children, we're displaying a preference for the childish.

"

Northwestern University commencement, Evanston, Illinois, US, June 2006

"

This democracy we have is a precious thing. For all the arguments and all the doubts and all the cynicism that's out there today, we should never forget that, as Americans, we enjoy more freedoms and opportunities than citizens in any other nation on Earth. **"**

University of Michigan commencement address, Ann Arbour, Michigan, US, May 2010

66

The true strength of our nation comes
not from the might of our arms or
the scale of our wealth, but from
the enduring power of our ideals:
democracy, liberty, opportunity, and
unyielding hope. **99**

Election victory speech, Chicago, Illinois,
US, November 2008

"

To be an American is about
something more than what we look
like, or what our last names are, or
how we worship. **"**

Address on immigration, the White House,
US, November 2014

66

No matter who you are or what you look like, how you started off, or how and who you love, America is a place where you can write your own destiny.

99

Speech following the Supreme Court ruling in favour of legalizing same-sex marriage, Washington DC, US, June 2015

"

The long sweep of America has been defined by forward motion, a constant widening of our founding creed to embrace all and not just some.

"

Farewell address, Chicago, Illinois, US, January 2017

66

It's important to recognize that the African-American community is looking at this issue through a set of experiences and a history that doesn't go away. **99**

Comments on the shooting of unarmed teenager Trayvon Martin, July 2013

66

When America gets a cold,
sometimes black folks get
pneumonia.

99

Conversation with *The Undefeated*,
North Carolina A&T State University, US,
October 2016

66

Everything we have done has been viewed through the lens of family … Beyond just the immediate family to the larger American family, and making sure everybody's included and making sure that everybody's got a seat at the table. **99**

Interview with *Vogue* magazine,
March 2013

66

We are and always will be a nation
of immigrants.

99

Address on immigration, the White House,
US, November 2014

6

LIFE &
FAMILY

Obama became well known during his presidency for his close relationships with his daughters Sasha and Malia, his wife Michelle, and even with his Vice President Joe Biden – a "bromance" that spawned numerous internet memes. He was open, too, about how the important people in his life made him not just a better President but a better man.

"

I am reminded every day of my life, if not by events, then by my wife, that I am not a perfect man.

"

Campaign rally, Mitchell, South Dakota, US, June 2008

66

It is absolutely men's responsibility to fight sexism too. And as spouses and partners and boyfriends, we need to work hard and be deliberate about creating truly equal relationships.

Column "This is what a feminist looks like" for *Glamour* magazine, August 2016

99

66

I would not be standing here tonight without the unyielding support of my best friend for the last sixteen years, the rock of our family and the love of my life, our nation's next First Lady, Michelle Obama.

99

Election victory speech, Chicago, Illinois, US, November 2008

66

To know Joe Biden is to know love
without pretence, service without self-
regard, and to live life fully. **99**

On presenting Joe Biden with the
Presidential Medal of Freedom, White
House, US, January 2017

66

After I received the news, Malia
walked in and said, 'Daddy, you
won the Nobel Peace Prize, and it
is Bo's birthday!' And then Sasha
added, 'Plus, we have a three-day
weekend coming up.' So it's good
to have kids to keep things
in perspective.   **99**

On winning the Nobel Peace Prize, the
White House, US, October 2009

"

When you're the father of two daughters, you become even more aware of how gender stereotypes pervade our society. You see the subtle and not-so-subtle social cues transmitted through culture. You feel the enormous pressure girls are under to look and behave and even think a certain way.

"

Column "This is what a feminist looks like" for *Glamour* magazine, August 2016

> **"**
> I miss Saturday morning, rolling out of bed, not shaving, getting into my car with my girls, driving to the supermarket, squeezing the fruit, getting my car washed, taking walks. **"**

Interview with Hearst Newspapers,
April 2011

66 Michelle will tell you that when we get together for Christmas or Thanksgiving, it's like a little mini United Nations. I've got relatives who look like Bernie Mac and I've got relatives who look like Margaret Thatcher. We've got it all. **99**

The *Oprah Winfrey Show*,
October 2006

"

It's important that their dad is a feminist, because now that's what they expect of all men. **"**

Column "This is what a feminist looks like" for *Glamour* magazine, August 2016

66

Michelle's like Beyoncé in that song. 'Let me upgrade ya!' She upgraded me. 99

Interview with *Vogue* magazine, March 2013

66

Joe's candid, honest counsel has made me a better President and a better Commander-in-Chief. From the Situation Room to our weekly lunches, to our huddles after everybody else has cleared out of the room, he's been unafraid to give it to me straight, even if we disagree — in fact, especially if we disagree.

99

On presenting Vice President Joe Biden with the Presidential Medal of Freedom, White House, US, January 2017

66

On my deathbed, I will not
remember any bills I passed, I will
not remember any speech I gave,
I will not remember getting the
Nobel Prize. What I will remember
is holding hands with my daughters,
taking them down to a park. **99**

Conversation with *The Undefeated*, North Carolina
A&T State University, US, October 2016

66

I made all kinds of bad decisions.
And so if that's true for me, that's true
for kids everywhere. **99**

Conversation with *The Undefeated*, North Carolina
A&T State University, US, October 2016

66

Michelle's had to accommodate
a life that, it's fair to say, was not
necessarily what she envisioned for
herself. She has to put up with me.
And my schedule and my stresses.
And she's done a great job on that.

99

Interview with *Vogue* magazine,
March 2013

66

There's no doubt I'm a better man having spent time with Michelle. I would never say that Michelle's a better woman, but I will say she's a little more patient. **99**

Interview with *Vogue* magazine, March 2013

"

I tease Joe sometimes, but he has been at my side for seven years, I love that man. He's not just a great Vice President, he is a great friend. We've gotten so close in some places in Indiana, they won't serve us pizza anymore. **"**

White House correspondents dinner, Washington DC, US, April 2015

66

Children need our unconditional love – whether they succeed or make mistakes; when life is easy and when life is tough. **99**

Weekly Address celebrating Father's Day, June 2011